T0039748

Passantino STUDENT PAD
NO. 15 EXTRA WIDE 6 STAVES

assantino STUDENT PAD
NO. 15 EXTRA WIDE 6 STAVES

 STUDENT PAD
NO. 15 EXTRA WIDE 6 STAVES

Passantino STUDENT PAD
NO. 15 EXTRA WIDE 6 STAVES

Passantino STUDENT PAD
NO. 15 EXTRA WIDE 6 STAVES

Passantino STUDENT PAD
NO. 15 EXTRA WIDE 6 STAVES

Passantino STUDENT PAD
NO. 15 EXTRA WIDE 6 STAVES

assantino STUDENT PAD
NO. 15 EXTRA WIDE 6 STAVES

assantino STUDENT PAD
NO. 15 EXTRA WIDE 6 STAVES

Passantino STUDENT PAD
NO. 15 EXTRA WIDE 6 STAVES

Passantino STUDENT PAD
NO. 15 EXTRA WIDE 6 STAVES

Passantino STUDENT PAD
NO. 15 EXTRA WIDE 6 STAVES

Passantino STUDENT PAD
NO. 15 EXTRA WIDE 6 STAVES

Passantino STUDENT PAD
NO. 15 EXTRA WIDE 6 STAVES

Passantino STUDENT PAD
NO. 15 EXTRA WIDE 6 STAVES

Passantino STUDENT PAD
NO. 15 EXTRA WIDE 6 STAVES

assantino STUDENT PAD
NO. 15 EXTRA WIDE 6 STAVES

Passantino STUDENT PAD
NO. 15 EXTRA WIDE 6 STAVES

Passantino STUDENT PAD
NO. 15 EXTRA WIDE 6 STAVES

Passantino STUDENT PAD
NO. 15 EXTRA WIDE 6 STAVES